CREATIVE  TOUCHES™

Papering Projects

ETC.

D0573217

THE HOME DECORATING INSTITUTE®

Copyright© 1996 Cy DeCosse Incorporated 5900 Green Oak Drive Minnetonka, Minnesota 55343
1-800-328-3895 All rights reserved Printed in U.S.A.

Library of Congress Cataloging-in-Publication Data Papering projects etc. p. cm. — (Creative touches) Includes index. ISBN 0-86573-877-7 (softcover)
1. House furnishings. 2. Paperhanging. 3. Wallpaper. 4. Textile fabrics in interior decoration. I. Cy DeCosse Incorporated. II. Series.
TT387.P367 1996 698'.6 — dc20 96-28584

CONTENTS

Wallcovering Basics

Wall Treatments

Furniture & Accessories

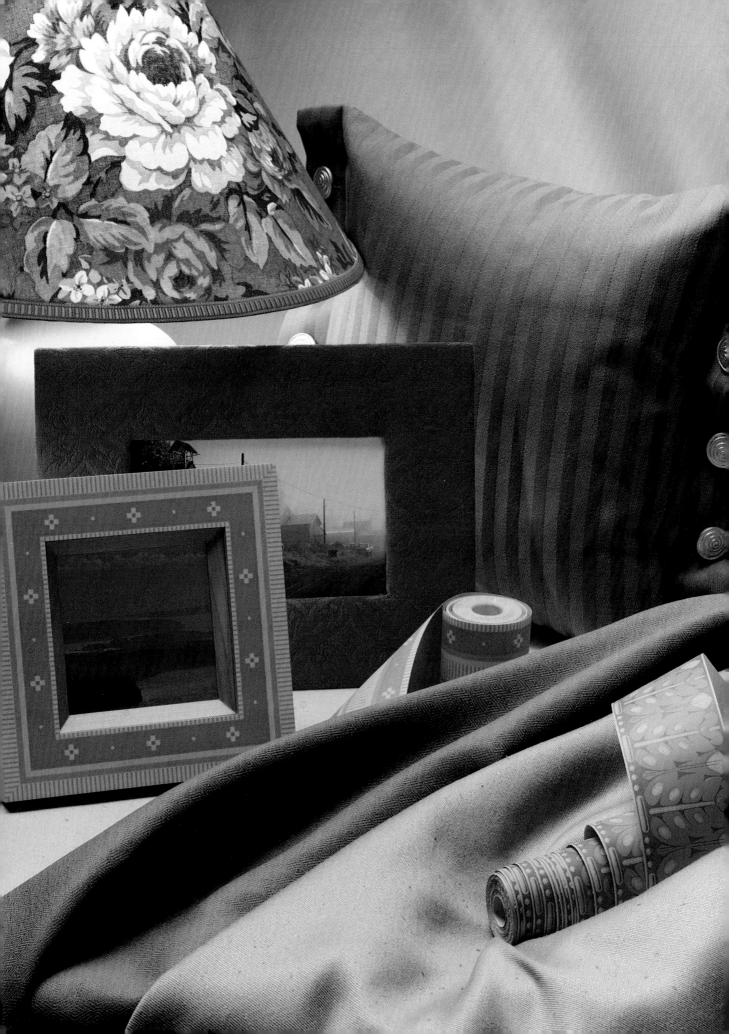

Papering Projects ETC.

Wallpaper has long been a recognized term used for the decorative covering applied to walls. Though in the past, these decorative coverings were indeed made of paper, today the broader term, wallcovering, is used to include other materials, such as vinyls and natural fibers.

Aside from papering entire walls, there are many creative uses for wallcoverings that can be accomplished in smaller projects. Wallcoverings can be incorporated into your decorating scheme to achieve a custom-designed look with professional results.

Wallcovering borders and cutouts can be applied in various ways to create interesting accents on walls. Isolated wallcovering panels break up expansive walls with decorative impact. Wallcovering borders make an effective chair rail or architectural accent.

Wallcovering can be applied to a cornice to create a custom-made window treatment. Motifs can be cut from wallpaper rolls or borders and applied to the flat surfaces of cabinets or furniture. Even lamp shades can be papered, adding pattern or texture to a room.

Easy techniques are explained with full-color photography, showing you countless ways to add creative touches with wallpaper.

Wallcovering Basics

Wallcoverings may be used in many creative ways to add interest and variety to a decorating scheme. Wallcoverings with different patterns may be combined to achieve unique effects. To find wallcoverings that work well together, look for patterns that have similar colors or design motifs rather than limiting yourself to patterns that are designed as coordinates.

After selecting a wallcovering, consult the salesperson about the proper adhesive. Many wallcoverings are prepasted and do not need additional adhesive. The paste on these wallcoverings is activated by dipping the wallcovering in water. Unpasted wallcoverings are applied using a clear vinyl adhesive. Border adhesive is often recommended for applying a vinyl border over a vinyl wallcovering; any excess border adhesive must be removed immediately, because it is impossible to remove after it has dried. Some wallcovering pastes may discolor painted surfaces and touching up may be required.

Before applying a wallcovering, clean the wall surface to remove any grease or soil. A solution of equal parts of ammonia and water works well. Repair any cracks or dents by filling them with spackling compound.

For some wallcovering applications, premixed sizing is recommended. This product prevents the adhesive from soaking into the wall surface. It also improves adhesion of the wallcovering and makes it easier to reposition, if necessary. Sizing is recommended for applications in humid areas. Once applied, sizing may be difficult to remove.

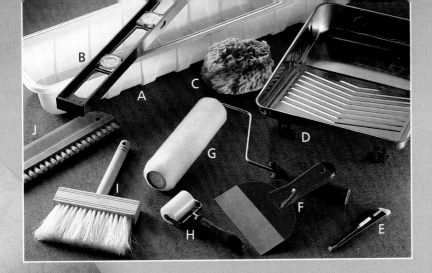

Tools required for papering projects include A. WATER TRAY for use with prepasted wallcovering, B. CARPENTER'S LEVEL, C. NATURAL SEA SPONGE, D. PAINT TRAY, E. RAZOR KNIFE with a breakaway blade, F. WIDE BROADKNIFE, G. PAINT ROLLER, H. SEAM ROLLER, I. PASTE BRUSH for applying adhesive to unpasted wallcovering, and J. SMOOTHING BRUSH.

How to prepare wallcovering

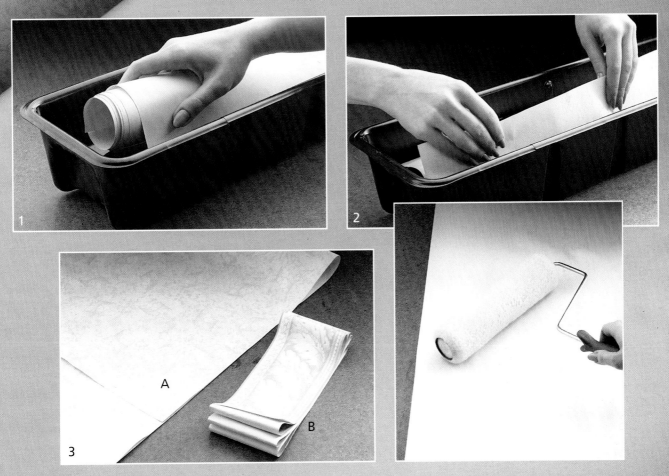

1. PREPASTED WALLCOVERING. Fill the water tray half full of lukewarm water. Roll the cut strip loosely, adhesive side out. Wet the roll in the tray as directed by the manufacturer, usually for about 1 minute or less.

2. Hold one edge of the strip with both hands, and lift the wallcovering from the water; check pasted side to make sure strip is evenly wet.

3. Cure short or vertical wallcovering strips by folding ends to center, pasted side in, without creasing folds (A); for long horizontal strips, fold the wallcovering strips accordion-style (B). Allow the strip to set for about ten minutes.

UNPASTED WALLCOVERING. Place the strip patterned side down on a flat surface. Apply adhesive evenly, using paint roller or paste brush. Wipe adhesive from table before preparing next strip. Cure strip as in step 3.

WALL TREATMENTS

Wallcovering Borders

Decorating with wallcovering borders is an easy way to add style to a room. Borders can be used to define a space, highlight architectural features, or add interest by creating new lines.

Available in a variety of designs, borders can be used to complement any decorating style. Designs include florals, geometrics, and architectural patterns. To achieve unique effects, borders can be cut apart or combined with other borders. For best results when using a border to outline or frame features of a room, select a border with a nondirectional print, because directional prints may not be pleasing when hung upside down. Some border designs are available with matching or coordinating corner pieces, which add a distinctive finishing touch. You can also make your own custom corner piece by cutting design motifs from wallcovering or wallcovering borders.

When determining the border placement, consider where the placement will draw the eye and what the placement will do to the proportions of the room. A border placed at the top of the wall draws the eye upward, providing a balance with elements at a lower level. Positioned at the picture rail level, a border visually lowers the ceiling. Consider running the border in a continuous band around doors and windows instead of ending the border when it meets the door and window moldings. For borders used as chair rails, position the center of the border one-third of the distance up from the floor on the wall surface.

When hanging borders, begin in an inconspicuous location. Plan the placement, if possible, so the more conspicuous corners are mitered evenly; corners at eye level or higher are usually more noticeable than lower corners. Where the last border segment meets the first, a mismatch usually results.

Wallcovering borders are available by the yard (m) or prepackaged in 5-yd. to 7-yd. (4.6 to 6.4 m) spools. To estimate the yardage needed, measure the areas where the border will be applied. Allow extra yardage for matching adjoining spools and for any damage that may have occurred to the ends of the rolls. Also allow at least twice the border width plus 2" (5 cm) for each mitered corner.

How to hang wallcovering borders

1. Cut first border strip, and prepare strip (page 7). Draw a light pencil line around room at desired height, using a carpenter's level, if positioning the border at location other than ceiling or baseboard.

2. Position border at the least conspicuous corner. Overlap the border around corner of adjacent wall for ½" (1.3 cm). Press border flat along wall with a smoothing brush; have an assistant hold folded portion of border while you apply and brush it.

3. Form a ¼" (6 mm) tuck just beyond each inside corner. Continue to apply border. Cut border at corner, using a sharp razor knife and wide broadknife.

4. Peel back the tucked strip, and smooth strip around the corner. Press the border flat. Apply seam adhesive to lapped seam, if necessary.

5. Overlap border strips so patterns match, if a seam falls in middle of wall. Cut through both layers, using a wide broadknife and a razor knife. Peel back border, and remove cut ends. Press border flat. Roll seam after 1/2 hour. Rinse adhesive from border, using damp sponge.

6. Trim border at a door or window frame by holding border against outer edge of frame with a wide broadknife and trimming excess with a sharp razor knife.

How to miter wallcovering borders

1. Apply the horizontal border strips, extending them past the corners a distance greater than the width of the border. Apply the vertical border strips, overlapping the horizontal strips.

2. Cut through both layers at a 45° angle, using a razor knife and a straightedge. Peel back the border; remove ends.

3. Press the border flat. Roll the seam after ½ hour. Rinse adhesive from seam, using a damp sponge.

TIPS FOR DECORATING WITH WALLCOVERING BORDERS

TRIM away upper or lower edges of the border along the lines of the design to create interesting effects.

MAKE borders economically by cutting standard rolls of wallcovering into border strips. Striped wallcoverings with nondirectional designs are especially suitable.

APPLY designs cut from borders over mitered corners to camouflage seams.

FINISH cut end of border with a strip of edging cut from additional length of border. Cut edging strip diagonally at corners to form a mitered appearance with edging on border.

More ideas for wallcovering borders

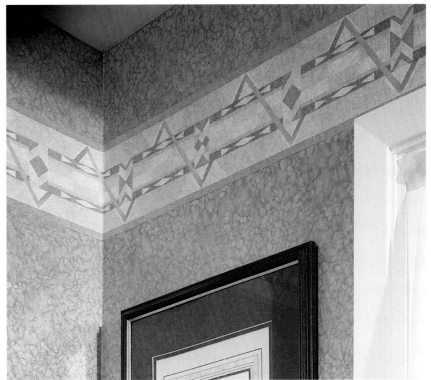

OPPOSITE: DOUBLE ROW OF BOR-DER STRIPS gives greater impact along the ceiling.

RIGHT: DECORATIVE BORDER is positioned about 2 ft. (0.63 m) below the ceiling to divide the wall.

BELOW: CEILING-LINE BORDER draws the eye upward. The lower portion of the border is cut away along the edge of the design to integrate the border and the painted wall.

Continued

More ideas for wallcovering borders
(CONTINUED)

TOP: COMBINATION OF BORDERS creates an interesting effect at the ceiling level.

RIGHT: VERTICAL BORDER STRIPS can be used to divide plain walls. The placement guidelines were marked using a carpenter's level and pencil. An edging strip cut from an additional length of border is used to finish the upper and lower edges. The edging strips are applied to the cut ends of the border as on page 15.

ABOVE: MITERED BORDER frames a
window. Design motifs from the border are
cut out and applied over the miters to camouflage the seams (page 15).

*W*allcovering Panels

Wallcovering and coordinating borders can be used to create decorative wall panels. The panels are less costly than covering entire rooms and add interest to otherwise plain walls.

Make panels to divide large walls into smaller sections, or use panels to highlight pictures and mirrors. The panels may be identical in size, or wide panels may be alternated with narrow ones. As a general rule, space the panels evenly on the wall, allowing slightly more space between the lower edge of the panel and the baseboard. Begin by planning the placement of the most dominant panels first. You may want to plan placement on graph paper, taking into account the position of any windows, doors, or built-ins. Also take into account any pattern repeat in the wallcovering to allow for matching patterns, if necessary.

How to make wallcovering panels

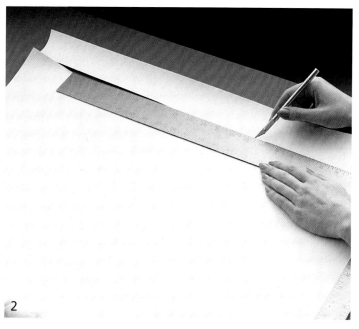

1. Determine the size and position of wall-covering panels by cutting and taping paper to the wall. Using a pencil and a carpenter's level, lightly mark the dimensions of the panel on the wall. Measure and record the dimensions.

2. Cut a strip of wallcovering for the center of the panel to size, using a framing square to ensure 90° angles at the corners. Prepare the wallcovering as on page 7.

3. Unfold the top portion of the prepared strip. Position lightly on the wall, aligning wallcovering with marked lines; use your palms to slide the strip in place. Press top of the strip flat with a smoothing brush, checking for bubbles, and reposition as necessary.

4. Unfold bottom of strip; use palms to position strip against marked lines. Press strip flat with smoothing brush, checking for bubbles.

5. Cut and apply any remaining strips, matching pattern and butting seams. Roll seam after 1/2 hour. Rinse any adhesive from the wallcovering and wall, using clear water and a damp sponge. Prepare border as for unpasted wallcovering (page 7), using border adhesive.

6. Apply border strips to panel in clockwise direction, starting at least conspicuous corner; align outer edge of border to edge of panel and allow ends to extend slightly beyond edges of panel. Miter corners as on page 14, steps 2 and 3; do not affix border firmly at first corner until final border strip is applied. Roll outer edges of border and seams after 1/2 hour.

More ideas for wallcovering panels

ABOVE: CEILING PANEL draws the eye upward. The placement lines for the panel were determined by measuring in 6" (15 cm) from each wall.

OPPOSITE: WALL PANEL creates a border around a painting. Companion corner pieces are used for additional interest.

RIGHT: GROUPING OF PANELS adds interest to a wall. The square panels near the base of the wall are centered under a long horizontal panel.

*W*allcovering Cutouts

Wallcovering cutouts are design motifs that are cut from wallcovering or borders. The cutout designs can be used to create interesting patterns or trompe l'oeil effects on painted walls. Unique designs can be created by combining motifs from different wallcoverings. For best results, walls should be painted with a high-grade washable paint, such as a low-luster or satin-sheen paint or a flat enamel.

For most wall applications, a clear vinyl adhesive will bond cutouts to the wall surface. If you are applying a border adhesive to prepasted cutouts, it may be desirable to remove the prepasted glue to reduce the thickness of the paper. Remove glue from prepasted wallcovering by soaking the cutout in water and lightly rubbing the pasted side. Blot the cutout with a towel to remove excess water; then apply the desired adhesive.

How to apply a wallcovering cutout

1. Cut wallcovering motifs using a mat knife and cutting surface or small, sharp scissors; simplify the designs as necessary. For easier handling, make any interior cuts before trimming outer edges.

2. Place the cutout facedown on a sheet of plastic or wax paper. Gently brush on a thin, even layer of adhesive, using a sponge applicator.

3. Press the cutout on surface; smooth out any air bubbles, using damp sponge. Roll the edges firmly with a seam roller. Rinse off any excess adhesive, using damp sponge.

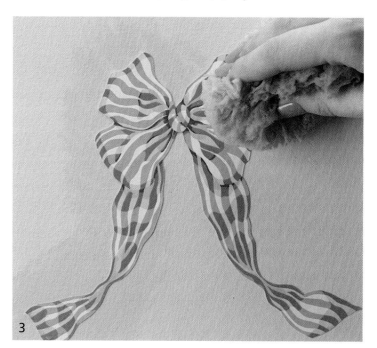

A

TIPS FOR DECORATING WITH CUTOUTS

Create a focal point with pictures or plates by using design motifs like ribbons or ropes as faux hangers (A). Mark position of the picture or plate first, then cut the wallcovering motifs for positioning above and below. The motifs need not continue behind the object.

Extend length of a motif by cutting it apart and spreading the sections (B). Fill in the space between sections with smaller designs, such as flowers, rosettes, or bows.

Plan placement by positioning cutouts temporarily with poster putty (C). Mark the positions lightly with pencil or use positioned pieces as a guide when securing each motif in place.

B

C

More ideas for wallcovering cutouts

OPPOSITE, TOP: TROMPE L'OEIL embellishes a kitchen wall. Plate, bowl, and vase motifs are cut from a wallcovering border and positioned above a shelf. Apple motifs and an edging strip, cut from a second border, help to unify the look.

OPPOSITE, BOTTOM: STORYBOOK SCENE is created by placing teddy bear motifs in the center of a wallcovering panel (page 21).

ABOVE: FLORAL ARCHWAY frames the upper portion of a window, for a feminine look.

RIGHT: HEADBOARD EFFECT is created by positioning cutouts on the wall above the bed.

FURNITURE & ACCESSORIES

Wallcovering on Furniture

Embellish tables and the flat surfaces of other furniture, such as trunks, dressers, and cabinets, with wallcovering to create distinctive furniture and accent pieces. For a quick embellishment, apply borders or cutouts. For a more intricate look, create your own custom design to imitate the look of tile or inlay. For this look, the wallcovering pieces are separated by narrow sections painted to simulate grout or spacers.

Tile or inlay designs can be as simple as cutting one wallcovering into squares or using several wallcoverings and more intricate pieces to create complex designs. Inlay designs are especially attractive when made from wallcoverings that imitate marble or stone. The paint chosen to imitate grout lines or spacers must be compatible with the surface being painted.

Wallcovering can be applied to most furniture surfaces, including metal, varnished, painted, and laminate. Apply the wallcovering using a border adhesive; this adhesive is suitable for all surfaces and ensures a strong bond.

To protect the wallcovering and to seal the edges, apply several coats of a clear finish, such as water-based polyurethane or acrylic finish, to the embellished surface. This finish can be applied over most surfaces and is easy to work with. For durability, select a finish that is recommended for surfaces that receive heavy use.

LEFT: INLAY DESIGNS on the coffee table and end table are made by cutting three different wallcoverings into design shapes. Spacer lines separating the shapes are painted gold.

How to apply wallcovering to furniture in a tiled or inlaid design

MATERIALS

- Wallcovering.
- Ammonia, for cleaning furniture surfaces.
- Fine-grit sandpaper, for deglossing shiny surfaces.
- Sheet of paper; transfer paper.
- Paint, for simulated grout or spacer lines.
- 1/4" (6 mm) tape, for marking simulated grout or spacer lines.
- Painter's masking tape.
- Border adhesive.
- Sponge applicator; sponge; seam roller.
- Mat knife or rotary cutter and cutting surface.
- Clear finish, such as water-based polyurethane or acrylic.
- Permanent markers or colored pencils, in colors to match the furniture surface or the edges of wallcovering, optional.

1. Measure the dimensions of the furniture, and plan the design on graph paper. Cut sheet of paper to design size, and mark points where design lines intersect. Use 1/4" (6 mm) tape and straightedge to mark grout or spacer lines on paper. It may be helpful to fold the paper into equal sections before marking design.

2. Prepare furniture surface as on page 38, step 1. Tape off outer edge of the design on furniture with painter's masking tape. Transfer any complex designs using transfer paper; simple designs may be transferred using straightedge and pencil.

3. Label top side of each design piece. Cut paper pattern apart along edges of tape lines; discard 1/4" (6 mm) tape strips. Tape pattern pieces to wallcovering, top side up; cut design pieces. The white cut edges of the wallcovering may be colored, using permanent marker or colored pencil that matches the furniture surface or wallcovering.

4. Paint over marked lines, applying paint wider than the 1/4" (6 mm) needed for grout or spacers; wallcovering pieces will partially cover the paint, leaving 1/4" (6 mm) between the pieces.

5. Position the wallcovering designs on the furniture surface; lightly mark placement lines. Complete the project as on page 38, steps 4 and 5; if the wallcovering expands after the adhesive is applied, trim pieces to size, using a mat knife.

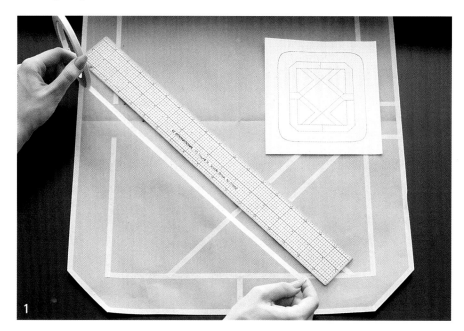

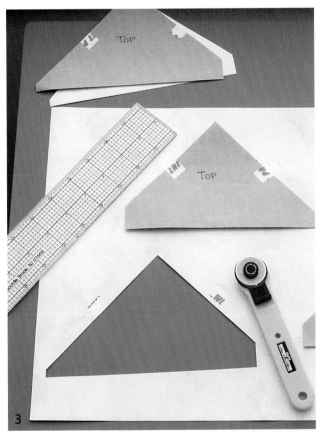

How to apply wallcovering border & cutouts to furniture

MATERIALS

- Wallcovering border and cutouts as desired.
- Ammonia, for cleaning furniture surfaces.
- Fine-grit sandpaper, for deglossing shiny surfaces.
- Border adhesive.
- Sponge applicator.
- Sponge.
- Seam roller.
- Mat knife and cutting surface, or small sharp scissors.
- Clear finish, such as water-based polyurethane or acrylic.
- Permanent markers or colored pencils, in colors to match the furniture surface or the edges of wallcovering, optional.

1. Clean furniture surface, using a solution of equal parts of ammonia and water, to remove any grease or soil. Degloss areas of shiny surfaces that will be covered with wallcovering, by lightly sanding with fine-grit sandpaper. This improves adhesion for the adhesive and clear finish.

2. Cut design motifs from wallcovering. White cut edges of wallcovering may be colored, using a permanent marker or colored pencil that matches furniture surface or wallcovering.

3. Arrange the designs on the surface as desired; lightly mark the position, using a pencil.

4. Apply an even coat of border adhesive to the back side of the wallcovering, using a sponge applicator. Press the wallcovering on the furniture surface; smooth out any air bubbles, using a damp sponge. Cut any mitered borders as on page 14; immediately roll the edges and seams of the wallcovering firmly with a seam roller. Allow to dry thoroughly.

5. Apply clear finish to the embellished surface, using a sponge applicator and following the manufacturer's directions; allow to dry. Repeat to apply three or more coats.

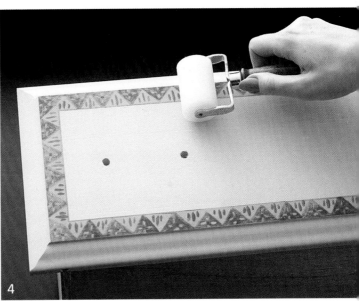

*More ideas
for wallcovering
on furniture*

LEFT: TABLE AND CHAIRS are embellished with wallcovering cutouts. Plate motifs cut from a border embellish the table. A floral motif cut from a different wallcovering decorates each chair back.

RIGHT: WALLCOVERING can be used to add design interest to ordinary furniture. A fruit basket wallcovering cutout creates a focal point on a desk. Wallcovering border edging strips outline the drawers and top of the desk.

BELOW: GAME TABLE is accented with wallcovering edged by a narrow rope border. Cards and chips were cut from a coordinating wallcovering.

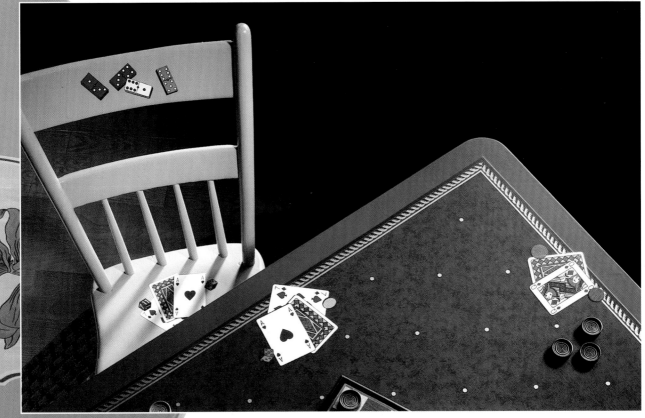

Continued

ABOVE: CHILDREN'S TOY CHEST is decorated with cars, trucks, and airplanes cut from a wallcovering border. Other wallcovering pieces are applied to the top and the lower edge of the chest.

OPPOSITE, TOP: CABINET has wallcovering applied to the inside of the door panels to create a trompe l'oeil effect.

OPPOSITE, BOTTOM: CHEST, painted with black paint, is embellished with Chinese-style motifs and border edging strips cut from wallcovering.

Cornices

Use wallcovering borders to create sleek, tailored cornices. These cornices are especially attractive when used with simple undertreatments, such as shades, blinds, and sheer curtain panels. For a finished look, paint the edges of the cornice to match or coordinate with the edge of the wallcovering border.

Determine the inside measurements for the cornice only after any undertreatment is in place. The cornice should clear the undertreatment by 2" to 3" (5 to 7.5 cm), and it should extend at least 2" (5 cm) beyond the end brackets for the rod on each side. Choose a wallcovering border that is wide enough for the completed cornice to cover any drapery heading and hardware.

MATERIALS

- ½" (3.8 cm) finish plywood with smooth finish on at least one side.
- Wallcovering border; border adhesive; sponge applicator.
- Wood glue; wood filler; medium-grit sandpaper.
- 16 × ½" (3.8 cm) brads; nail set.
- Primer suitable for paint and wallcovering.
- Paint to coordinate with or match the edge of the wallcovering border.
- Angle irons; pan-head screws or molly bolts.

CUTTING DIRECTIONS

Measure and cut the plywood for the top piece of the cornice to correspond to the inside measurements of the cornice, as necessary for the clearance of the undertreatment. Cut the cornice front piece to the expanded width of the wallcovering border (below). The cut width of the cornice front is equal to the width of the cornice top plus two times the thickness of the plywood. Cut the cornice side pieces equal to the expanded width of the wallcovering border by the depth of the cornice top.

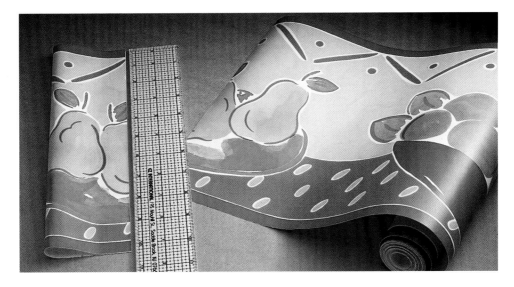

DETERMINE the expanded width of the wallcovering border by applying border adhesive to a 6" (15 cm) length of border. Fold the border in half; allow to set about 5 minutes, then remeasure the width. This is the actual height to cut the cornice front and side pieces.

How to make a cornice

1. Glue and nail each side piece to the top piece, aligning the upper edges; secure with nails. Glue and nail the front piece, aligning it to the top and side pieces. Countersink nails. Fill the nail holes with wood filler; fill front, sides, and lower edges of plywood as necessary. Sand front and side surfaces and edges smooth.

2. Apply primer; allow to dry. Paint lower edges and top of the cornice, extending paint slightly over edges to front and sides; paint inside of cornice.

3. Cut wallcovering border equal to distance around the sides and front of the cornice plus 4" (10 cm). Prepare wallcovering as for unpasted wallcovering (page 7), using border adhesive. Center wallcovering on cornice, wrapping wallcovering around the back edge of cornice just to the inside edge of plywood; trim excess paper.

4. Secure angle irons on inside of cornice top, near ends and at 45" (115 cm) intervals or less. Hold cornice at desired placement, making sure it is level; mark the screw holes on wall or window frame. Remove angle irons from cornice. Secure angle irons to wall, using pan-head screws drilled into wall studs, or use molly bolts. Reattach the cornice to installed angle irons.

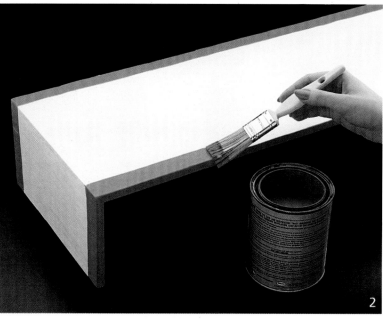

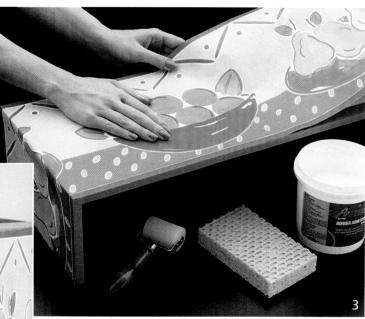

More ideas for cornices

ABOVE: BORDER EDGING STRIP, cut from a companion wallcovering border, trims the upper and lower edges of a shaped cornice.

OPPOSITE, TOP: SCALLOPED BORDER is used to create a cornice with a shaped lower edge. The scallops are cut, using a jigsaw with a fine-toothed scroll-cut blade.

OPPOSITE, BOTTOM: STACKED BORDERS add height to this cornice.

Lamp Shades

Make a customized lamp shade to coordinate with the decorating scheme of any room. Choose from either pleated or unpleated styles. Both versions use a purchased smooth lamp shade as a base.

For a pleated wallcovering shade, select a wallcovering or border that easily holds a crease, such as a paper-backed vinyl wallcovering. For an unpleated lamp shade from wallcovering, avoid using a wallcovering that has a striped or plaid pattern.

How to make a pattern for an unpleated lamp shade

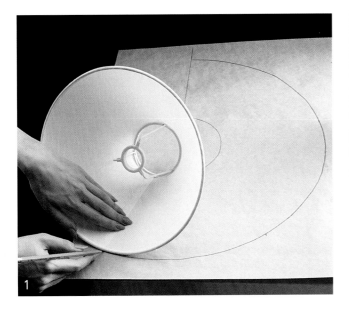

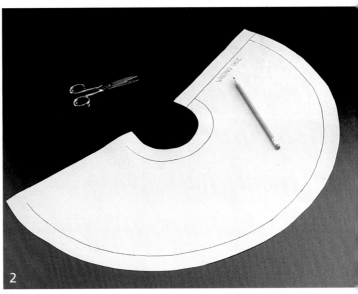

1. Mark a line, longer than the height of the lamp shade, on a large sheet of paper. Position lamp shade on paper, aligning seam of shade to the marked line. Roll lamp shade, and trace upper edge of shade to seam, using pencil; realign lamp shade seam with the marked line. Roll lamp shade, and trace lower edge of shade to seam.

2. Cut out paper pattern, allowing 1″ (2.5 cm) excess paper around all edges. Label the pattern for wrong side of shade cover.

Continued

How to make a pattern for an unpleated lamp shade

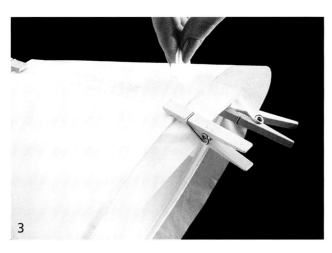

3. Position pattern on lamp shade, wrong side of pattern toward shade, aligning marked line to seam on shade; clamp, using clothespins. Tape ends together. Check fit of pattern, and redraw lines as necessary.

4. Remove the pattern; cut on straight line marked in step 1. Fold the pattern in half; crease. Mark crease for the lengthwise or crosswise direction of the wallcovering. Trim upper and lower edges of pattern, ⅝" (1.5 cm) from marked lines.

How to make an unpleated wallcovering lamp shade

MATERIALS

- Wallcovering.
- Smooth plastic or paper lamp shade, for base.
- Border adhesive; sponge applicator.
- Narrow trim, such as gimp or braid.
- Thick craft glue.
- Clothespins; sponge.

1. Make pattern (page 51). Position the pattern, wrong side down, on right side of wallcovering. Trace around pattern, adding ⅜" (1 cm) at one short end, for overlap. Cut on the lines marked on wallcovering.

2. Apply border adhesive to one-quarter of the lamp shade, starting about 3" (7.5 cm) from seam. Place cover on shade, aligning short end of cover with seam of shade; upper and lower edges will extend ⅝" (1.5 cm) beyond the edge of shade. Smooth out any air bubbles or wrinkles in the wallcovering. Continue to apply the wallcovering to the remainder of lamp shade, working with one-quarter section at a time; overlap the wallcovering at seam of shade. Remove any excess adhesive, using a damp sponge.

3. Continue to apply wallcovering to remainder of the lamp shade. Working with one-quarter section at a time, overlap wallcovering at seam of shade. Remove any excess adhesive, using damp sponge.

4. Make ½" (1.3 cm) clips, at ½" (1.3 cm) intervals, along upper edge of shade and at wire spokes. Fold wallcovering to inside of shade; secure, using border adhesive. Clamp the wallcovering in place as necessary with clothespins; allow to dry.

5. Make ½" (1.3 cm) clips, at ½" (1.3 cm) intervals, along lower edge of shade. Fold wallcovering to inside; secure with border adhesive, easing in extra fullness. Apply narrow trim to the upper and lower edges, to conceal edges of wallcovering; secure with thick craft glue.

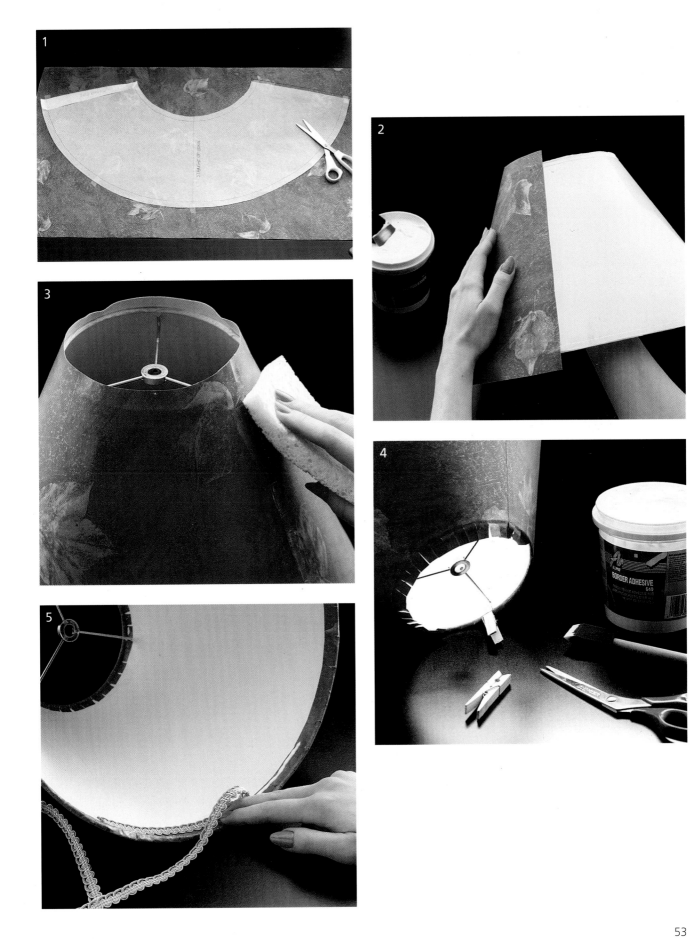

How to make a pleated wallcovering lamp shade

MATERIALS

- Wallcovering or wallcovering border, about ¾" (2 cm) taller than height of lamp shade.
- Smooth plastic or paper lamp shade, for base.
- Thick craft glue or hot glue gun and glue sticks.
- Transparent ruler.
- Soft elastic, about 1" (2.5 cm) wide, optional.
- String; plastic-coated paper clips.

1. Measure the height of the lamp shade along the sloped side; add ¾" (2 cm) to this measurement to determine cut width of the wallcovering. Measure the shade circumference at the lower edge; multiply by 2½ to determine the cut length of the wallcovering. Cut the wallcovering to these measurements.

2. Mark a light pencil line on the wrong side of the wallcovering, parallel to and 1" (2.5 cm) from the upper long edge of the strip. Repeat at the lower edge. Mark pleat lines within the marked lines, spaced 1½" (3.8 cm) apart and parallel to the short edges.

3. Fold the wallcovering on pleat lines, creasing sharply. Align adjacent pleat lines, and crease to fold crisp ¾" (2 cm) accordion pleats.

4. Overlap short ends of pleated wallcovering; trim excess wallcovering. Divide pleated wallcovering and shade into fourths at upper edges; mark, using paper clips.

5. Secure pleated wallcovering into tightly folded bundle, using string; cushion the bundle with narrow strips of wallcovering to prevent marking the wallcovering. Set aside for several hours to set pleats.

6. Overlap the short ends of the pleated wallcovering, and secure, using thick craft glue; allow to dry.

7. Position pleated wallcovering over lamp shade, matching marks. Adjust pleats so they are even and extend about ½" (1.3 cm) above shade. Elastic, cut to fit around upper and lower edges of shade, may help to control fullness while position of pleats is adjusted.

8. Secure pleated wallcovering to lamp shade at upper and lower edges, using thick craft glue or hot glue. Allow to dry.

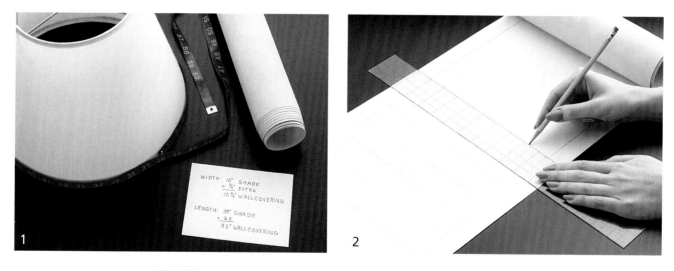

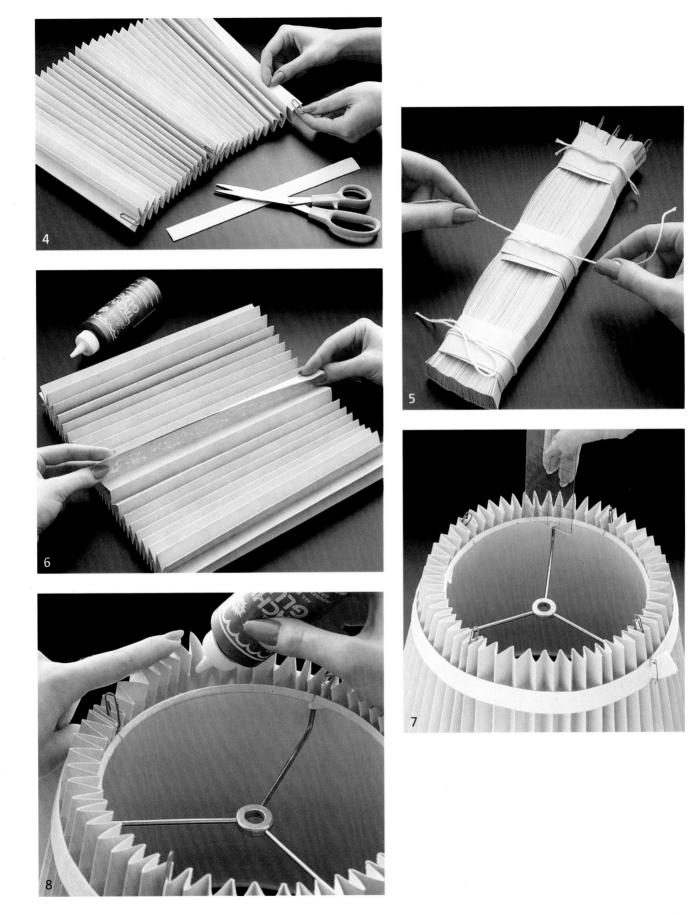

*H*eadboards

Create a custom headboard by securing wallcovering to a wooden base, trimmed with corner molding. Additional decorative moldings can be added, if desired. The headboard is wall-mounted with sawtooth hangers, eliminating the need for attaching the headboard to the bed frame.

The width of the headboard is equal to the width of the bed frame plus an allowance for the bedding. The height of the headboard is about 20" to 24" (51 to 61 cm). A rectangular base is recommended for the headboard, for ease in mitering the corner molding. Make a paper pattern of the headboard, and place it on the wall behind the bed. Check the size and shape, and adjust as necessary. You may also want to locate the wall studs and mark their locations on the pattern.

When choosing wallcovering, select solid vinyls for the most durability; these will not absorb skin and hair oils. To avoid seams, select a wallcovering that can be applied horizontally.

How to make a wallcovering headboard

MATERIALS

- ¾" (2 cm) particleboard, cut to shape.
- Wallcovering and wallcovering border.
- Wallcovering primer; border adhesive.
- Wallcovering tools as needed (page 7).
- 1⅛" (2.8 cm) corner molding, for framing headboard.
- Decorative moldings, optional.
- ⅞" (2.2 cm) finishing nails; nail set.
- Miter box and backsaw.
- Paint, or stain and matching putty, for molding.
- Wood glue; fine-grit sandpaper.
- Large sawtooth picture hangers.
- Two 1½" × ¾" (3.8 × 2 cm) corner braces.

1. Apply wallcovering primer to particleboard; allow to dry. Paint or stain the back side of the particleboard, if desired.

2. Prepare the wallcovering as for unpasted wallcovering (page 7), using border adhesive. Apply wallcovering to particleboard, trimming edges even with edge of board. Position molding on upper edge of the headboard; mark inside edge of molding, using pencil. Repeat for sides. Prepare wallcovering border, and apply to upper edges and sides, lapping border ⅛" (3 mm) beyond marked lines; miter corners as on page 14.

3. Miter the corner molding for sides of headboard at upper corners, using backsaw and miter box; leave excess length on the molding strips. Miter one corner on moldings for upper and lower edges of headboard, leaving excess length.

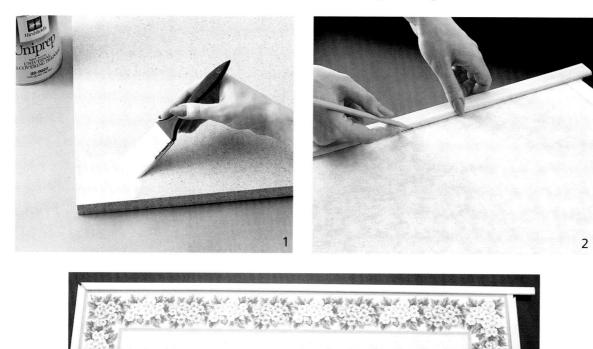

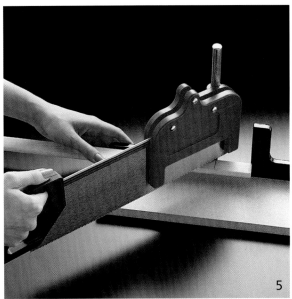

4. Position upper and side molding strips in place. Mark the angle of the cut at finished length of upper piece. Cut on marked line, using backsaw and miter box.

5. Reposition moldings. Mark finished length and angle of cut for each side piece; cut moldings on marked lines.

6. Position the lower molding, aligning mitered corner. Mark the finished length and angle of cut; cut miter. Reposition the moldings; sand the mitered corners, if necessary, for proper fit.

7. Paint or stain moldings as desired. Apply bead of glue to the molding, and position on the headboard. Use glue to secure mitered ends of moldings. Secure moldings to headboard, using finishing nails; predrill nail holes with 1/16" drill bit.

Continued

How to make a wallcovering headboard
(CONTINUED)

8. Countersink finishing nails, using nail set. Fill the holes with putty to match the stain, or touch up with paint.

9. Secure two to four sawtooth hangers to the back of the headboard, slotted edge down; position to align with wall stud locations, if possible.

10. Secure corner braces to lower edge of headboard, positioning one near each end. Hang headboard on wall, using sawtooth hangers. Secure corner braces to wall. Use molly bolts, if hangers and corner braces do not align with wall studs.

More ideas for headboards

RIGHT: WALLCOVERING CUTOUTS are used as accents on a wallcovering headboard. Apply the cutouts as on pages 28 and 29.

BELOW: WALLCOVERING BORDER is used horizontally at the upper edge of a headboard. Decorative painted finials are secured on each end of the headboard. Predrill the holes for the finials through the corner molding and particleboard.

Index

CY DECOSSE INCORPORATED

President/COO: Nino Tarantino
Executive V.P./Editor-in-Chief: William B. Jones
Chairman Emeritus: Cy DeCosse

Creative Touches™
Group Executive Editor: Zoe A. Graul
Managing Editor: Elaine Johnson
Editor: Linda Neubauer
Associate Creative Director: Lisa Rosenthal
Senior Art Director: Delores Swanson
Art Director: Mark Jacobson
Copy Editor: Janice Cauley
Desktop Publishing Specialist: Laurie Kristensen
Sample Production Manager: Carol Olson
Photo Studio Services Manager: Marcia Chambers
Publishing Production Manager: Kim Gerber

President/COO: Philip L. Penny

PAPERING PROJECTS ETC.
Created by: The Editors of Cy DeCosse Incorporated

Also available in the Creative Touches™ series:

Stenciling Etc., Sponging Etc., Stone Finishes Etc., Valances Etc., Painted Designs Etc., Metallic Finishes Etc., Swags Etc.

The Creative Touches™ series draws from the individual titles of The Home Decorating Institute®. Individual titles are also available from the publisher and in bookstores and fabric stores.

Printed on American paper by:
  R. R. Donnelley & Sons Co.
99 98 97 96 / 5 4 3 2 1

Cy DeCosse Incorporated offers a variety of how-to books.

For information write:
  Cy DeCosse Subscriber Books
  5900 Green Oak Drive
  Minnetonka, MN 55343